JELLICOE
AT SHUTE

JELLICOE
AT SHUTE

MICHAEL SPENS

A·D· ACADEMY EDITIONS · **E·S** ERNST & SOHN

Editorial Offices
42 Leinster Gardens, London W2 3AN

Photographic Credits
All colour photographs by Jamie Gardiner-Hill unless
otherwise stated. All black and white photographs by Susan Jellicoe.
Planting surveys on pp64-75 made and drawn by Lucy Whitaker.

Cover: *Lilies contrasting with rhododendrons marking the Spring.*
Back Flap: *Michael Spens (left) with Sir Geoffrey Jellicoe (right).*
page 2: *Upper Lake, View towards the Canal.*
page 6: *The Bog Garden.*

First published in Great Britain in 1993 by
ACADEMY EDITIONS
An imprint of the Academy Group Ltd

ACADEMY GROUP LTD
42 Leinster Gardens, London W2 3AN
ERNST & SOHN KG
Hohenzollerndamm 170, 1000 Berlin 31
Members of the VCH Publishing Group

ISBN 1 85490 265 2 HB
ISBN 1 85490 266 0 PB

Distributed to the trade in the United States of America by
ST MARTIN'S PRESS
175 Fifth Avenue, New York, NY 10010

Printed and bound in Italy

CONTENTS

THE GARDEN AT SHUTE
PREFACE BY GEOFFREY JELLICOE

Nearly sixty years ago I designed the great classical gardens of Ditchley Park, Oxfordshire, for Ronald and Nancy Tree. In due time their son Michael married Lady Anne Cavendish (of Chatsworth) and together they settled in the classical Mereworth Castle in Kent. Some twenty-five years ago they acquired Shute House and over the period have developed between them a garden that breaks through classicism into a landscape created with deeper aspects of human nature.

My own part in this has been that of a professional who endeavours to turn thoughts and ideas into reality.

Highpoint, Highgate
17 August 1993

THE BACKGROUND STORY

In the late years of the 1970s, Geoffrey Jellicoe entered a key transitional period in his long career as a designer of landscapes. Major works had of course been accomplished in the previous decade. Indeed, he had established a large staff to deal with his numerous clients, both institutional and private, and to implement their commissions. Ever since the 1940s his reputation had grown as the leader in the field.

Even before that, following the early patronage first by the American Anglophile Ronald Tree MP and his wife Nancy at Ditchley Park, Oxfordshire (1935), and subsequently the Bowes-Lyon family at St Pauls Walden Bury, Hertfordshire (1936), and the Duke and Duchess of York (later King George VI and Queen Elizabeth) at Royal Lodge, Windsor (1936), Jellicoe had become renowned, at least among an influential circle in England, for his talent with gardens and landscape.

Even before that, through the enlightened patronage of Viscount Weymouth, later the Sixth Marquis of Bath, he had been enabled to design an outstanding modernist building in the 1930s, the restaurant and visitors' centre at Cheddar Gorge in Somerset. On that project, Russell Page had assisted, as skilled a plantsman as Jellicoe was a designer.

During the 1930s Jellicoe's fame also spread as a teacher at the Architectural Association School of Architecture in London, and with no less than Maxwell Fry as runner-up, he was elected Principal in 1939. However, the mould had been set long before, and his destiny predicated as a landscape architect. In 1925 he published *The Italian Gardens of the Renaissance*, with a fellow Architectural Association graduate JC (Jock) Shepherd, as a fifth year student dissertation[1]. Thus at the age of twenty-five Jellicoe was already a name in his chosen field. These researches had implanted in Jellicoe's mind a deep and abiding appreciation of the scale, proportion, composition and indeed the philosophy of the Renaissance garden. This turned him towards landscape design. The publication led the Trees to him, and gradually further clients.

ABOVE: The Restaurant at Cheddar Gorge. A much prized early commission for Geoffrey Jellicoe. His design of 1934 was influenced by Erich Mendelsohn's De La Warr Pavilion, Sussex, of the same period. Jellicoe's work of the period was subsequently noted by Henry Russell Hitchcock Jnr in the exhibition of Contemporary Architecture held at the Museum of Modern Art, New York (1939) and more recently, the respected land-scape historian Tom Turner is quoted as saying: 'Jellicoe's building for the Cheddar Caves was widely illustrated in the 1930s as a pioneer modern building. Outside the restaurant he designed the first wholly modern garden in England' (Building Design, 11 December 1987). The Cheddar Gorge buildings were unfortunately restored unsympathetically in the 1960s and today show little trace of the original work.
OPPOSITE: View down the Lake at Shute showing the rhododendrons at the Spring Source and the Mop-Headed Acacia.

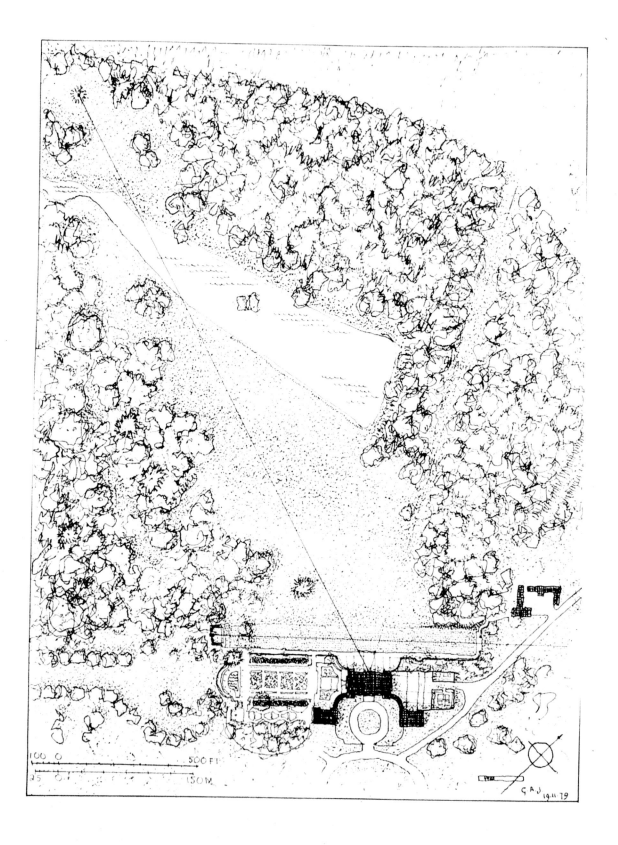

100 0   500 FT

25 0   150 M.

G A J 19.11.79

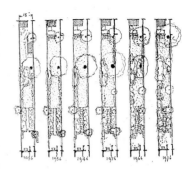

A curious inhibition affected Jellicoe from his student days with Jock Shepherd, a superlative architectural draughtsman whom Jellicoe felt he could never emulate on the drawing board. It was Jellicoe who paced out all the garden surveys, while Shepherd drew them up. No, Jellicoe felt that he could not draw proficiently (even though the evidence of the childhood sketchbooks runs counter to this impression). Even as late as the project design for the surrounds to the Royal Shakespeare Theatre, Stratford-on-Avon (1971) there is evidence of this imprecision.

But in fact the recovery began earlier, in an important garden design for Horsted Place, Sussex (now destroyed) for Lady Rupert Nevill (1965). The project designs demonstrate a growing pleasure in ink line itself as the most direct medium for the representation of woodland, beds, lawns and indeed water. Only here there is another riddle, no water exists at Horsted: it is represented by the fluidity of paths and beds which float across a lake of grass in Jellicoe's drawings. For water, in all its amazing variety, was ultimately to become the key formative element in Jellicoe's ensuing oeuvre.

In 1978 Geoffrey Jellicoe officially retired. Indeed, at seventy-seven, the prospect of a somewhat more relaxing life had seemed most inviting to both Susan and Geoffrey Jellicoe. They still inhabited the house and garden at Number 19, Grove Terrace in Highgate, North London, and at last it seemed that they might actually have time to enjoy the place. Jellicoe could look back with satisfaction on a long list of successfully completed projects in architecture and landscape, together with the knowledge that he had been a leading and formative influence in the proper establishment of the landscape profession, firstly in the United Kingdom and subsequently in the world at large. In the following year there was to come due and timely recognition of this very British public achievement, with the award of a knighthood.

But in fact 1978 was no marker for Jellicoe's retirement. The release from normal office pressures was in effect more of a dramatic catalyst for him, and suddenly he was able to devote time each day to reflection. And through the concentration on deeper issues Jellicoe began to develop his philosophy in a more profound manner than ever before. Of course his genesis of thought had already been distilled into print: the *Landscape of Man* (1975) became, and remains a basic guide to landscape thinking from the earliest times[2] and *Studies in Landscape Design*, which was published in textbook

ABOVE: Grove Terrace, Highgate. Plan series drawn by Geoffrey Jellicoe showing five decades of transition in the garden.
OPPOSITE: Ditchley Park. The commission for this 1936 design by Geoffrey Jellicoe came from Michael Tree's parents, Ronald Tree MP and Mrs (Nancy) Tree. Jellicoe produced a neo-classical design closely related to the house's Palladian inspiration (as designed in 1720 by James Gibbs).

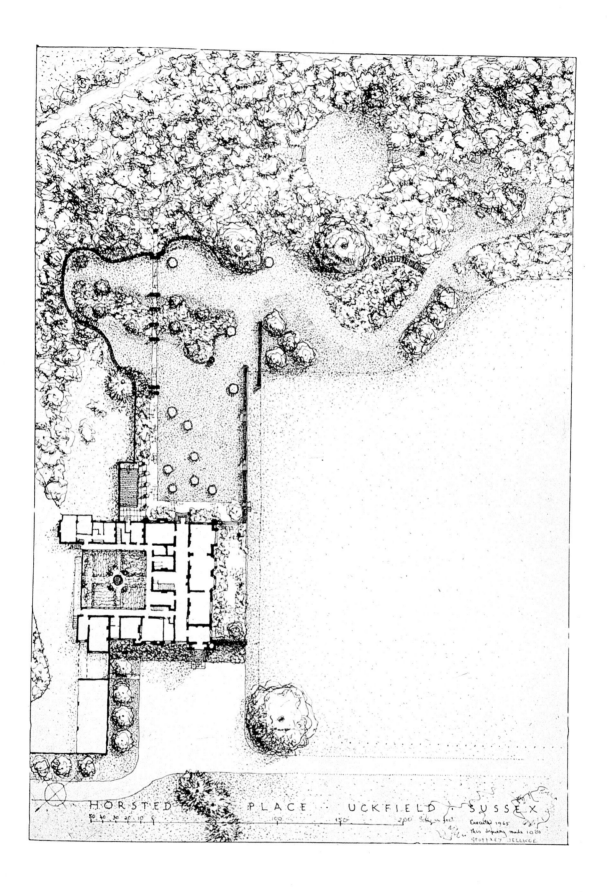

HORSTED · PLACE · UCKFIELD · SUSSEX

format in three volumes (1960/1966/1970) and remains to this day the only vocational publication of its kind.[3]

However, through the 1970s there had been no practical manner in which Jellicoe could develop the relationship between landscape design and philosophy on site, over a period of years. In the manner of the great landscape designers of the eighteenth century and their patrons (such as Hoare at Stourhead), Jellicoe urgently needed continuity on a single site. Above all else landscape is an art of the seasons, ephemeral in its palette of materials.

In 1969 Geoffrey Jellicoe at last received the go-ahead from Michael and (Lady) Anne Tree to draw up a full scheme for Shute – he had already been consulted earlier in the decade over the purchase. Shute, as will be shown, proved to be the answer to all Jellicoe's yearnings. Shute was to become the laboratory of his dreams.

BELOW: Elevation of the Cascade, Villa Torloni, Frascati, as described and drawn by Jellicoe and Shepherd in The Italian Gardens of the Renaissance *(London 1925) now republished in a facsimile edition by Academy Editions (1986).*
OPPOSITE: Horsted Place, Sussex. Design drawing by Geoffrey Jellicoe: 'starting from the house as from a quay these inanimate objects drift on their green river to disappear into the woods, apparently drawn to the parent circle secreted within.' (Geoffrey Jellicoe, Guelph Lecture, 1983.)

HOW IT BEGAN

In 1968 Michael and Anne Tree acquired Shute. Prior to that they had lived at Mereworth Castle in Kent. This superb English Palladian mansion had been possibly the finest project of the Scots Palladian architect Colen Campbell, and the drawings take pride of place in his work. The gardens there were appropriately formal, and in due course the Trees felt that they needed to be able to develop their own plans. There was no scope for change at Mereworth, and when they had previously invited Jellicoe to consider such opportunities as existed there, he wisely deferred on the basis that nothing further could be done to Campbell's creation or its surroundings.

But when the Trees duly showed him Shute, he was first intrigued and then greatly attracted to its inherent potential as a landscape garden. The house was early eighteenth century with origins well over a century earlier, and possibly much more ancient foundations. It loomed high over the adjacent public lane, straddling the ridge leading to Donhead St Mary like some Fiesolean villa. The landscape fell away both across the fields to the north, and more dramatically to the south. Here, instead of a distant view of the Duomo in Florence, the landscape swept up again to finally embrace the Downs. The view was redolent of ancient England; a landscape made by man indeed, but over millennia, not centuries. The existing gardens were not in bad shape and had been maintained in a manner more or less appropriate to the house of Shute. Jellicoe realised from the first that there was one wholly rare and original asset that above all lent Shute its special quality. At the western end of the grounds an ancient primaeval spring source bubbled gently. Jellicoe liked to quote Shelley's 'Lines Written in the Vale of Chamonix, Mont Blanc':

> The everlasting universe of things
> Flows through the mind, and rolls its rapid waves,
> Now dark – now glittering – now reflecting gloom
> Now lending splendour, where from secret springs
> The source of human thought its tribute brings
> Of waters – with a sound but half its own,
> Such as a feeble brook will oft assume . . .

OPPOSITE: Shute House viewed from the east. The house abuts closely to the village road. Jellicoe designed a new garden wall providing greater privacy, just visible to the right.

Jellicoe concurs with Shelley's identification of the self with the universe, and his instinctive reaching for a fourth and a fifth dimension. At Shute, this gentle movement was in fact the source of the Wiltshire river Nader. From this mysterious, moss-bottomed pool, hemmed in by a strange combination of rhododendrons, foxgloves and several species of fern, a steady flow issued in two directions: firstly to a retaining pool which appeared to be the main designated reservoir for the garden; and then via a stronger stream, downhill, and so out of the garden altogether to be lost in the buttercup-strewn meadows below. But Jellicoe was captivated by the mysteries of the spring, a name and a watercourse so ancient even in this historic part of England that its origins were lost in time. He realised that this feature alone offered a remarkable potential in gardening terms, moreover one that had hardly been tapped at all. For Jellicoe and the Trees were seeking something indefinable, yet very much more than a touch of the picturesque.

Thus Shute came into new ownership and in the space of less than twenty years it would be so changed as to become one of the most outstanding of twentieth-century English gardens. The Trees were to devote the prime of their lives to the place; at Shute, providing one had vision, ideas and energy there was a scene waiting for transformation. They and Jellicoe were to comprise an ideal triumvirate. Michael Tree was already an artist of recognised talent; Anne, with Chatsworth in her blood, was a skilled plantswoman and Jellicoe made sure that he would be at hand. At last for a brief period he was less sorely pressed by clients and anticipating a congenial retirement. Shute was a project of just the right scale for him to pursue over several years. At last he would distil, in one location, the essential truths of half a century of experience. It was a formidable prospect.

ABOVE: Anne Tree with Geoffrey Jellicoe on the lawn at Shute (1969). OPPOSITE ABOVE: The Landscape Setting for Shute. View north from the Downs in the vicinity of the ancient Icknield Way, the earliest cross-country route from Devon to Norfolk. OPPOSITE BELOW: Shute House from the south.

ABOVE: *The Spring Source of the River Nader.*
OPPOSITE: *Shute House, the initial Survey Drawing by Jellicoe indicating the existing layout in 1970 before work started.*

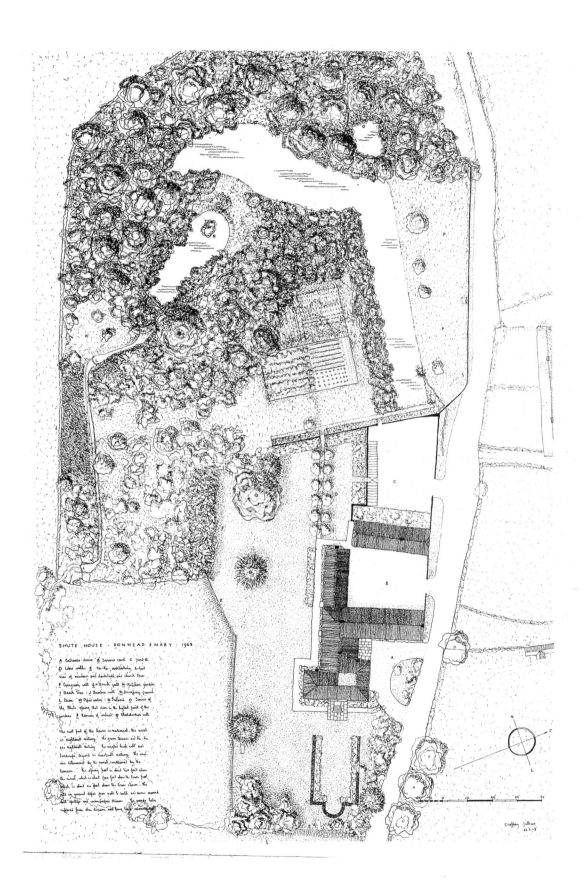

ABOVE: The Pools beyond the Spring. These were carefully placed to receive the flow after leaving the gardens.
OPPOSITE: Drawing showing the Spring Source which lies at the top of the entire water scheme at Shute.

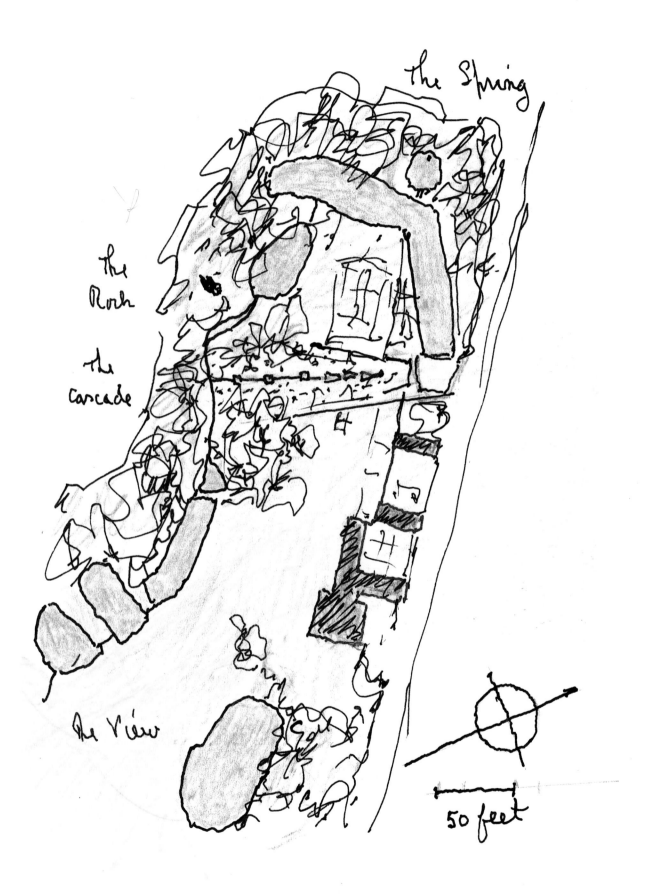

the Spring

The
Rock

the
Cascade

the View

50 feet

THE CONTROLLING ELEMENT
A TREATISE ON WATER

It is important first to address the key role that water is seen to play in Jellicoe's formal language of landscape design. In reviewing the seemingly endless progression of his projects, one finds that there had been less than a dozen schemes involving a relationship with water prior to Shute's inception. By contrast, in the decade and a half since then, some twenty have emerged. Overall, from Ditchley Park onwards, until the grand project for Atlanta, over thirty of Jellicoe's schemes have relied upon the presence of water in some form or other.

In 1971, following the completion of his three volume work *Studies in Landscape Design*, Geoffrey Jellicoe published his own illustrated treatise on the subject – *Water: The Use of Water in Landscape Architecture* (co-written with Susan Jellicoe).[4] This was the first study by a practising landscape architect to establish the importance of the element in the hierarchy of devices historically available to the designer of landscape and gardens.

> Whether we are watching the ceaseless movement of the waves
> on the seashore or the eddies on the surface of a pool, or reflections
> on a calm day, the fascination of water seems endless.

So wrote Jellicoe. At Rustington in Sussex, where he had spent most of his childhood, the English Channel beach had a marked effect, defined into sections by rows of sturdy timber breakwaters that deepened the perspective as they stretched into the distant haze of summer. Jellicoe draws an early distinction in his book between 'water in action' and 'contemplative water', claiming here that quietness and action are the essence of all water design. 'The historic culmination of contemplative water,' he says, 'was the artificial lake of the English school of landscape gardening.'

Here Jellicoe also places great emphasis on the idea of water. A great admirer of the constructivist sculptor Naum Gabo, he sees his manipulation of water through sculpture as highly significant in the modern age. Jellicoe is also greatly intrigued here by the extent to which the properties of illusion in art can be successfully sustained through the use of water. He refers specifically to the Shinto Japanese Itsukushima shrine (AD 811) dedicated to three daughters

OPPOSITE: View down the Canal to the three Classical Busts.

SHUTE: SKETCH FOR END OF CANAL

ELEVATION AS FROM SEAT

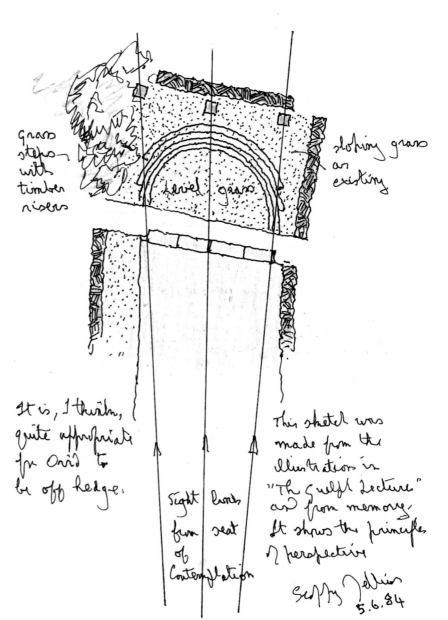

grass steps with timber risers

level grass

sloping grass as existing

It is, I think, quite appropriate for Ovid to be off hedge.

Sight lines from seat of Contemplation

This sketch was made from the illustration in "The Guelph Lecture" and from memory. It shows the principle of perspective

Geoffry Jellicoe
5.6.84

of Susano-No-Mikoto, a Shinto god, where the main shrine and its many connected subsidiaries appear, at high tide, to float without support on the waves. Mindful perhaps of the Ryoan-ji sand garden, Kyoto (AD 1499), Jellicoe used water as the theme of a composition wholly without actual water resources at Horsted Place (1964), as has been mentioned, and here it is grass, not sand, which is the contemplative 'water'.

Where active water is required, Jellicoe invokes the Moghul gardens of Kashmir, with special reference to the gardens of Shalamar and of Achabal (c1620). At Shalamar Jellicoe admires the manner in which the watercourse gradually descends the gradient in a series of waterfalls. In England, he admires the passive water of the Dutch inspired canal at Westbury Court, Gloucestershire (1697-1705) and notes the marked importance of the hedges lining its banks.

Accordingly it will be seen here that Jellicoe draws inspiration at Shute from a number of instances in the history of gardens: from Kashmir, from Japan and from Italy too. The sequence of water courses at the Villa Lante had made a lasting impression; the rill especially: 'expressing the elegance as well as the fun of water'. And at the Villa d'Este, Tivoli:

> the gardens are justifiably famous, for they are a stupendous achievement in water design. The waters of a substantial river were diverted and now pass through the gardens which hang on a steep hillside, so that the visitor feels he is engulfed in the movement, sound, and spray of water.[5]

When work began on the transformation of the long reservoir at Shute into an Italianate canal, the stage was set for a grand consummation of the spirit of water, and there was to be no turning back from then on. Like joyful conspirators, Michael and Anne Tree urged Jellicoe onwards into the fuller exploitation of this primaeval site and its undoubted potential.

OPPOSITE RIGHT: Design Sketch by Jellicoe of the canal's climax (dated 5 June 1984), indicating how the position of the busts is adjusted in perspective as seen from the two-way seat at the far end of the canal, opposite the spring.
OPPOSITE LEFT FROM ABOVE: Itsukushima Shrine, Japan (AD 811 and later) – the group of shrines preserve the illusion of floating on the sea surface when the tide is full; Ryoan-ji Sand Garden, Kyoto (AD 1499) – the sea of 'nothingness' in which the rocks have been placed is not of sand but of the beautiful, luminous quartz from the nearby river; Moghul Garden, Achabal, Kashmir (c1625) – a source of inspiration at Shute; The Water Rill at the Villa Lante, Bagnaia, Italy (1560) – the rapid movement of water down to the lower level garden creates the impression of appearing out of woods. The rill at Shute derived from several historical sources, Lante being a favourite Italian site for Jellicoe; The Water Theatre at the Villa d'Este, Tivoli – Jellicoe is impressed by the way the fullest use is made of gravity and contour.

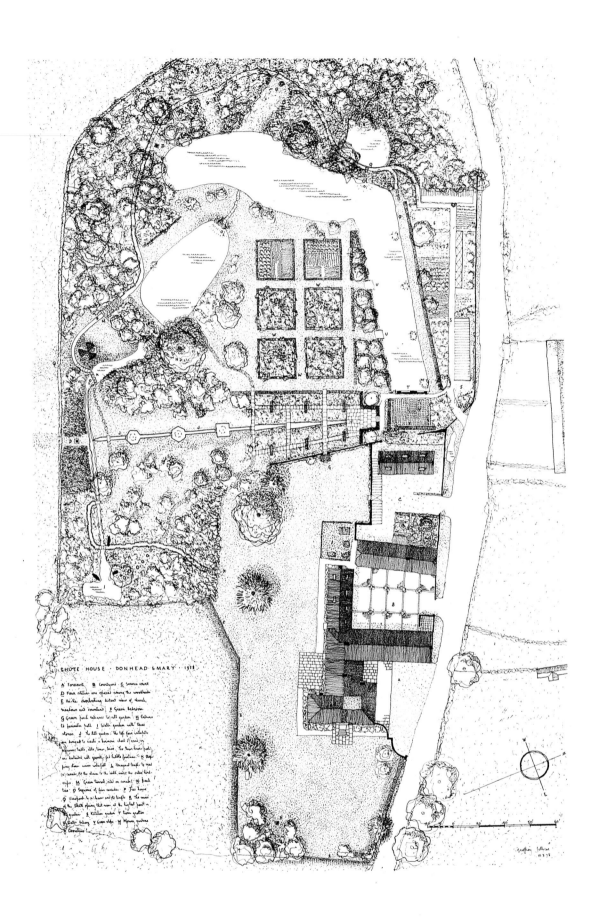

THE GARDEN LAYOUT AT SHUTE

The design for Shute, it must be remembered, was a rare example of team work, a collaboration between three rare individuals following a long friendship (in Michael Tree's case since childhood when Jellicoe designed Ditchley Park's formal gardens for his parents). Previously, Susan Jellicoe had tended to complete the actual planting layouts for Geoffrey, but here she 'stood down' so to speak, confident that the three collaborators had an adequate pool of talent and knowledge between them to succeed in their combined operations. Jellicoe, for his own part, did not however deviate from his normal practice of seeking to get at the real – as contrasted to the supposed – intentions of his clients. Shute was essentially a well harmonised collaboration.

> When I design a garden for a particular client, it is rather like painting a portrait; you have to get inside the clients' minds, and translate their wants through your art. That art contains a lot of things the layman can't understand or do; it's the abstract which lies behind all art . . . [which] everybody has within them, a certain creative power, and nearly everybody has an urge to get back to nature. At Shute, all tradition said that water was the key . . . the point to which the eye is drawn. But at Shute . . . I made water the subsidiary. I split the water into two ponds, with the view beyond. . .[6]

Such is Geoffrey Jellicoe's summary of the essence of the whole composition of this waterscape, as he calls it. Later, he was to expand on this description, in a special article prepared for the Museum of Modern Art, New York, at their request:

> The landscape, before alteration, like the house, was a complex of romantic charm. Water from the spring flowed downward through dense woodlands along the way feeding water shapes made at different dates for different purposes and finally flowing into a partially obscured scene of distant Downs along which ran an ancient way across Southern England. There was never any doubt that it was the thought, presence, act and sound of water that was holding together the competing ideas that had

OPPOSITE: The Final Scheme as developed 1970-93. Many elms had to be cleared, having died previously or as work continued. The changes made by Jellicoe were relatively contained, but crucial in turning an uninspiring conjunction of wilderness and threatened beds (centre) into a poetic experience where water was the vital element. The manner in which new paths were inserted to make the whole garden accessible is clearly evident, as is the removal of a small approach avenue leading from the house. The cascade is of course the single most vital innovation, a skewer linking the whole experience dramatically together.

been introduced into the woodlands – ideas remotely associated with Islam, Greece, the Middle Ages, the primaeval and other times and cultures. It was not until the summer of 1988, when the view was opened up and an abstract design of a further pool introduced, that a unity of earth and sky became apparent.[7]

Once this water course has emerged from the mysteries of the earth itself, it is guided by Jellicoe through a whole series of events across the gradually sloping contours. The spring burbles into the upper pool. From here water spreads languidly eastwards, scarcely mobile in the Italianate canal, with each side distinct from the other: to the north, lilies throng the shallow grassy edge in profusion; to the south, a tall hedge, in the seventeenth-century Dutch manner, runs its full length, punctuated only by two discrete wooden balconies, which give a reassuring clue about real scale. At the end of the long canal, we find – observed even from the seat by the spring itself – three busts set on pedestals, gleaming white. Closer inspection reveals them to be likenesses, or perhaps commemorations would be more accurate, of Jellicoe's favourite Augustan Roman poets: Virgil, Ovid and Lucretius.

Emphasising inherent ambiguities, so prevalent in art and in philosophy, a second flow of water issues from the upper pool, and joins a second, more southerly pool of a more deliberately picturesque connotation. Here stand two special figure statues, brought from Mereworth by Michael Tree.

Thus the underlying structure of the garden at Shute is generated. From this duality emerges the whole character of the garden. Continuing along the canal, one is obliged to pass the three poets and their backdrop, a miniature amphitheatre, before stooping low to pass through a triangular 'philosophers' grove' deeply planted with ilex trees. After the confident humanism of the canal, this grove is passed on one side, with something of a question mark to the observant visitor; but one emerges into an organised box garden. Here the visitor has to pause.

Approaching from the house itself in the first instance, as is normal, one passes through an opening in the stone wall, to find oneself standing at the head of the long rill, where a continuous sound of variegated waterfalls is apparent. In summer the rill is surrounded by a lush proliferation of growth. The rill, of course, is fed from the canal, and water follows the shortest and fastest route down the hill. In Jellicoe's prescribed route this has to be a foretaste, however. For the rill is an event to be perceived twice en route, and crossed on each occasion. Only latterly is there opportunity to walk up or down either side.

The path of the water courses is of course subsidiary to the path which the visitor must follow. But at Shute the various aspects of the waterscape constitute the primary experience intended.

The visitor has now followed the initial path from the spring along the canal; has passed the ilex grove, and stands by six box beds, which offer a remarkable mixture of annual, perennial and wild plants. The route now runs downhill past a superb mop-headed acacia tree (planted by Anne Tree), towards the latest area of innovation: the allegorical garden. Here Jellicoe deliberately creates a space to confront man's superstition of the unknown, mixing classicism and romanticism like the sorcerer's apprentice. The approach is through a green laurel tunnel, so low that one has to stoop to pass through. Here is a temple in miniature . . . this is no Grecian or neo-classical construct however, but something infinitely more pagan from beyond the Urals, a fantasy structure in the design of which Anne Tree has also been closely involved. Now almost wholly clad in ivy, it provides

OPPOSITE: The Three Busts of Ovid, Virgil and Lucretius.

ABOVE: Mereworth Figure Sculpture in a Classical Setting.

ABOVE: The 'Philosophers' Grove', as designated by Jellicoe. This occurs at a key angle in the sequence where the visitor must move from the canal across to the box beds (or vice versa); Jellicoe felt this acute angled 'elbow' to be crucial as a transitional experience. The rows of ilex trees are crossed by separate paths projected at right angles from the box beds beyond, and so the canal balconies recognise this angle.
PAGE 32 ABOVE: Figure Sculpture from Mereworth. The positioning is such that is can be viewed from several angles as the vantage point changes en route. The 'romantic' setting is pivotal as distinct from the canal climax to the north, which is essentially a single view.
BELOW: The Mop-Headed Acacia. Planted by Anne Tree this accentuates the range of green foliage beyond, with its rather lighter shades.
PAGE 33: Into the Box Garden. The passage opens out into a disciplined garden, an evidently productive area in contrast to the cerebral nature of the ilex grove.

a standpoint from within which the distant prospect of the bog garden can be surveyed. It seems too, that this allegorical garden is intended to be visited as the shadows lengthen, preferably on a late summer evening, when dusk is stealing in. Then salvation may come in a quick dash homewards, past the now more measured flows at the base of the rill, through the spectacular foliage of the bog garden, and with due acknowledgment to its silent, African sentinel. The lights of Shute House provide a final beacon of reassuring domesticity as the visitor scuttles in below a large cedar tree: pausing for just a moment to take in the meaning of the outdoor 'spare bedroom' and its double bed of box hedge, set aside for latecomers.

BELOW: The Temple Garden. Plan drawn by Geoffrey Jellicoe (20 June 1985).
OPPOSITE: View up the Cascade, from below to the south.

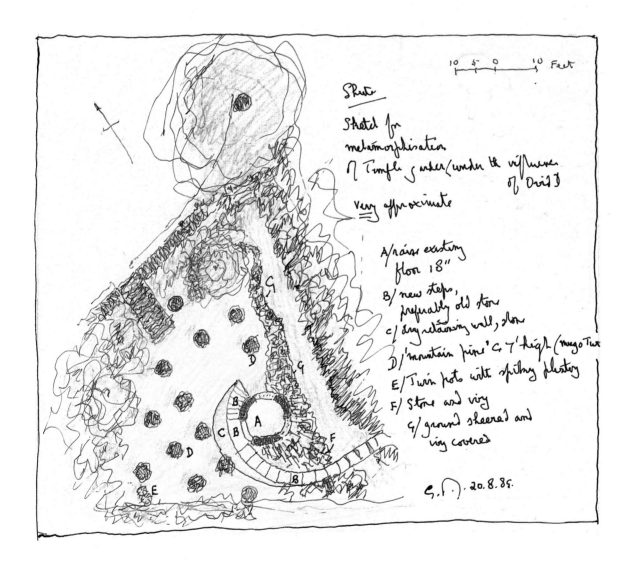

ABOVE: The Laurel Tunnel, exit point, arrival in the Temple Garden.

ABOVE: The Temple Garden. The temple completed.

ABOVE: The Bog Garden. This stone sculpture from Zimbabwe (c1985) marks the entrance.
OPPOSITE: Anne Tree's Guest Bed for tardy guests late back from the gardens.

THE GARDENS IN DETAIL
A DESCRIPTION BY GEOFFREY JELLICOE

Geoffrey Jellicoe has written his own description of the gardens at Shute, in which he chooses an anti-clockwise sequence to demonstrate that the path can work in either direction chosen. His description is given again here, complete with further comments on his subsequent developments.[8] The garden is divided into some eight main areas, 'seven or more green compartments having been devised for the romantic, semi-watery wilderness that lay behind the wall'.

THE CANAL

Anti-clockwise the perimeter path leads through clipped hedges to the straight canal. In the distance is the cascade from the hidden pool, the source of the water. The path passes behind the grottos and along the canal, giving glimpses of the inner garden through the water balconies. The canal turns and the scene changes from the classical to the romantic, another sculpture from Mereworth being seen beyond the water against dark trees and foliage. The path plunges into the woodlands and arrives at the two-way seat of contemplation, one part looking outwards towards the house and the other inwards to what the Greeks would undoubtedly have designated the 'sacred' spring.

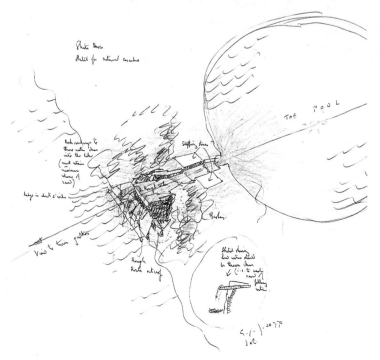

LEFT: The Spring Source. Design sketch by Geoffrey Jellicoe (1970) for the water transition from spring to pool. OPPOSITE: The Water Coursing beyond the Spring. PAGE 42: The Water Balconies. Each balcony is an identical projection of a path in parallel from the box garden. The angle of the balconies is adjusted to the line of the canal. PAGE 43: The Water Balconies give scale to the canal perspective.

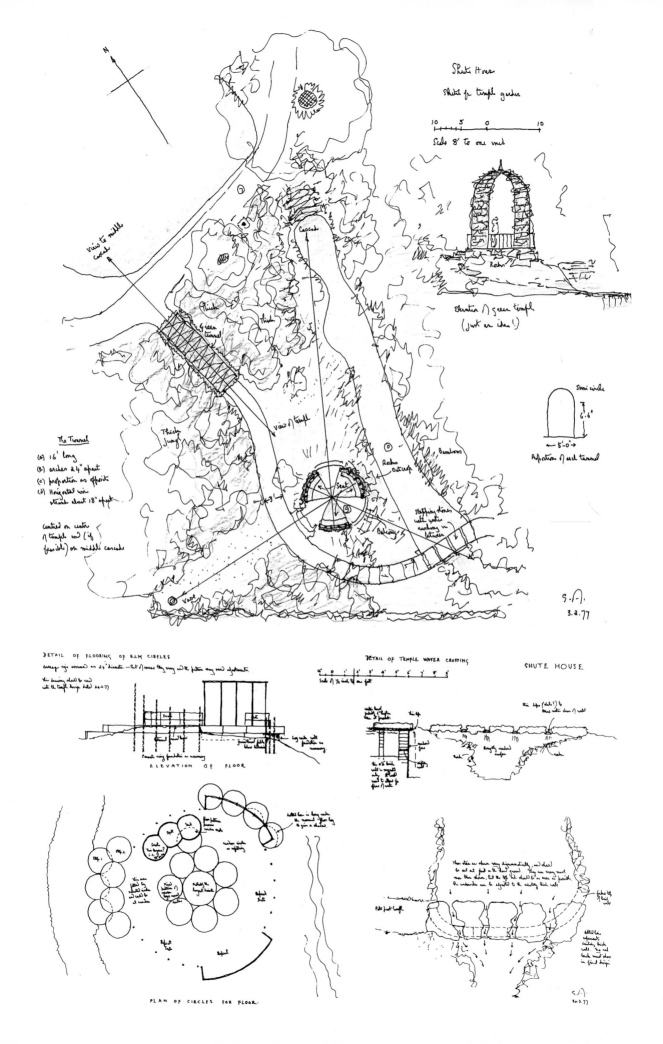

Shute House

Sketch for temple garden

10 5 0 10

Scale 8' to one inch

Elevation of green temple
(just an idea!)

View to middle
cascade

Green tunnel

Plinth

Cascade

View of temple

The Tunnel

(a) 16' long
(b) arches 24" apart
(c) proportion as opposite
(d) horizontal wire
stained about 18" apart

centred on centre
of temple and (if
feasible) on middle cascade

Thick jungle

Seat

Balcony

Rocks outcrop

Bamboos

Stepping stones
with water
running in
between

Vase

Semi circle

6'-6"

5'-0"

Proportion of each tunnel

G.A.
3.2.77

DETAIL OF FLOORING OF ELM CIRCLES

DETAIL OF TEMPLE WATER CROSSING

SHUTE HOUSE

ELEVATION OF FLOOR

PLAN OF CIRCLES FOR FLOOR.

G.A.
30.3.77

THE TEMPLE

The path continues through woodlands with two accidental glimpses of the garden across water. You emerge beside a lower lake and plunge immediately into a green tunnel. Beyond, in a small exclusive enclave in the woods and open to the agricultural landscape beyond, is a hexagonal ivy temple.

This is the second step backward in time. One balcony overlooks the dark recesses of the largest of the cascades and the rivulet below, another looks towards the outer landscape, and the third (in due course) to the present-day equivalent of a mythological urn. You leave this temple by hazardous stepping stones across a lower cascade – hazardous because no eclectic landscape can be complete without an element of peril, real or imaginary.

THE TEMPLE GARDEN (REVISED)

Lady Anne brought a rock crystal to catch the rays of the setting sun and she wanted to put it somewhere remote and mysterious to be a 'magic' stone. I had previously designed a temple garden with a quasi-gazebo made of unclipped ivy, approached through a green tunnel. Lady Anne and I evolved the idea of mystical shapes made of clipped yews. It should be a place where a child might be slightly frightened. Already the iron skeletons which will form the base for topiary are on site – abstract chessmen, perhaps, or still figures from another planet. Not a place for the timid on a dark night.

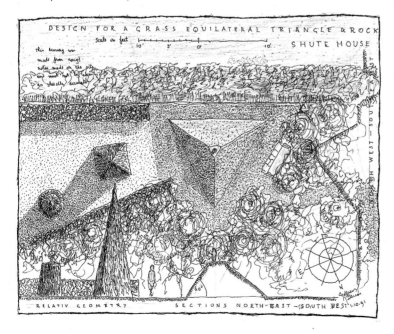

LEFT: Jellicoe's Unrealised Design for the installation of a Rock Crystal Block in the vicinity of the Temple Garden (1 October 1991).
OPPOSITE ABOVE: The Temple. Jellicoe's design of 1977, one of several versions discussed with the Trees.
OPPOSITE BELOW: The Temple. Design details of the pavings of circular elm cuttings and of the water crossing beyond.

ABOVE: The Temple Garden. Iron frames for the 'figure' trees. The entrance is to the right.

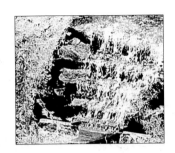

THE BOG GARDEN

After threading your way through foliage and crossing the lower end of the rill, you enter the bog garden in which three great stones are set. The long journey in time ends with one of the oldest ideas in the relation of man to environment – the Chinese philosophy of an analogy between man and the rock from which he emerged, and the human significance of the stone itself. Three stones were chosen for their personality from a nearby disused quarry, and . . . were disposed on the site in a relationship that was unaccountably agreeable.

THE STEPPED CASCADE IN DETAIL

The water from its source in the highest pool finds its way southwards by two routes, one classical (canal and rill) and the other romantic (lower pool and temple), the two re-uniting before entering the bog garden. The three cascades of the romantic route are formed from stones selected from the adjoining quarry. The stones of the upper cascade were chosen for their horizontality and the specification for positioning was so simple that they were constructed by a local stonemason with an instinctive understanding of what was required.

THE APPLE PORCH

This is the entrance to woodland gardens that are small and compartmented in space, but eclectic in time. With water, foliage and trees as building materials, the mind is invited to experience the complexities of classicism and romanticism, finding satisfaction in the unity of these two seeming opposites and traditional antagonists.

THE RILL

There is water in abundance, embarrassingly so when it emerges from countless subterranean streamlets, but nevertheless, the cause of abnormal fertility. The sound of water [is] everywhere, intensified by altogether eleven small falls or cascades. The first four of [the] eight chutes of the rill itself are designed to form a harmonic chord of treble, alto, tenor and bass; but whether such an idea is unique is debatable, for any water sound would be pleasing in such a setting. In the distance is a sculpture, brought from Mereworth Castle. . .

The bubble fountains . . . are gravity worked, an idea derived from Kashmir. Behind the small viewing terrace at the summit of the cascades there was planned a conservatory inspired by that which once existed at Chatsworth (well known to Anne Tree) having an

ABOVE: The Stepped Cascade, detail of operation.
PAGE 48 ABOVE: The Spring Source, origin of the whole experience.
PAGE 48 BELOW: The Bog Garden.
PAGE 49: The Apple Porch, entrance from the house lawns. Passage through the wall is direct, signified by the iron portico now fully covered with foliage, and gateless.

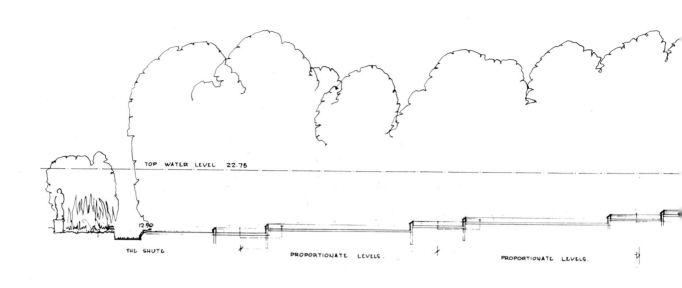

TOP WATER LEVEL 22.75

THE SHUTE   PROPORTIONATE LEVELS.   PROPORTIONATE LEVELS.

NOTE
THE SETTING OUT DEPENDS
UPON THE RELATION OF
ASH TREE TO SCULPTURE
AS FOLLOWS.

SPRING FLOWERS IN DRIFTS
UNDER TREES.
NO FORMAL PATHS.

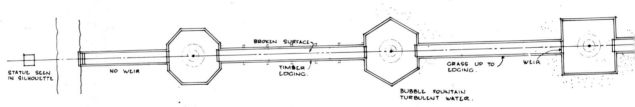

STATUE SEEN   NO WEIR   BROKEN SURFACE   GRASS UP TO   WEIR
IN SILHOUETTE   TIMBER   LOGING.
                                     LOGING.
                          BUBBLE FOUNTAIN
                          TURBULENT WATER.

SPRING FLOWERS IN
DRIFTS UNDER TREES.

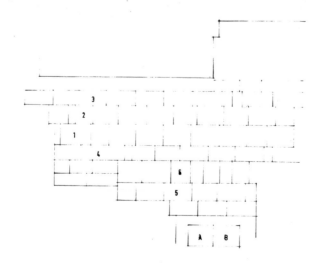

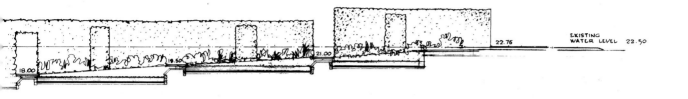

EXISTING
WATER LEVEL 22.50

22.76

21.00

19.50

18.00

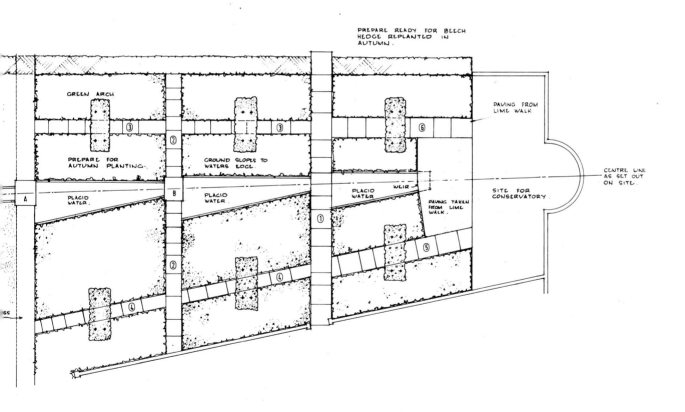

PREPARE READY FOR BEECH
HEDGE REPLANTED IN
AUTUMN.

GREEN ARCH

PAVING FROM
LIME WALK

③

③

⑥

PREPARE FOR
AUTUMN PLANTING.

GROUND SLOPES TO
WATERS EDGE.

CENTRE LINE
AS SET OUT
ON SITE.

②

PLACID
WATER.

PLACID WATER.

PLACID
WATER

WEIR

SITE FOR
CONSERVATORY.

A

B

①

PAVING TAKEN
FROM LIME
WALK.

②

④

⑤

④

④

SS

SHUTE HOUSE : HALF FULL SIZE OF CHUTE 1. (TREBLES)

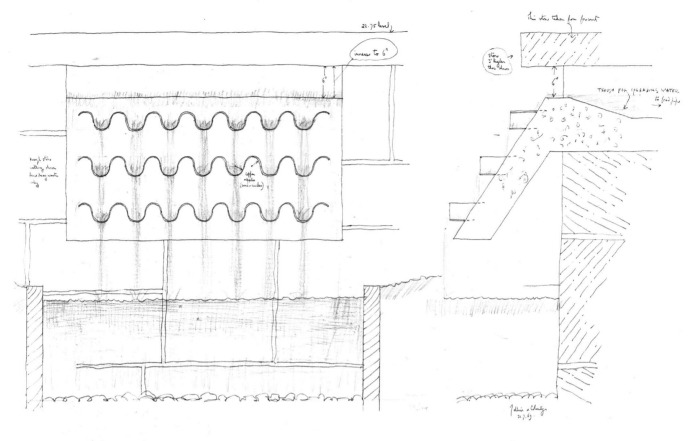

SHUTE HOUSE : HALF FULL SIZE OF CHUTES 2, 3, & 4

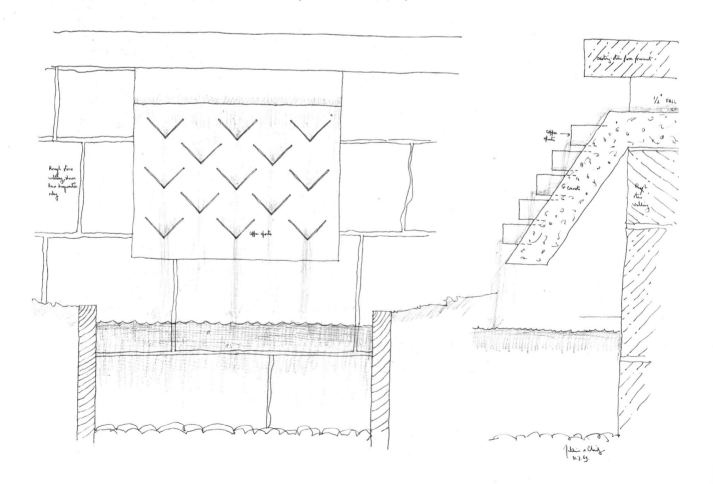

ABOVE: The Cascade. Stone Slabs.
PAGES 50-51: The Cascade. Initial measured design drawing from the office of Jellicoe and Coleridge setting out the Jellicoe plan for the full installation (June 1969).
PAGE 52 ABOVE: The Cascade. Detail by Jellicoe of the arrangement of 'trebles' (1969).
PAGE 52 BELOW: The Cascade. Detail by Jellicoe of alto, tenor and bass elements (1969).
PAGE 53: The Cascade. The view down (to the south) with the Mereworth figure sculpture at the end.
OPPOSITE ABOVE: The Alto Cascade. Detail of operation.
OPPOSITE BELOW: The Stepped Cascade. Detailed sketch by Jellicoe for all masonry works (10 December 1973).

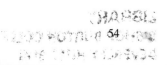

interior of moss or fern walls all kept continuously damp. The realisation of this would have proved too costly in structure and maintenance, and its place as crucial to the composition has been taken by clipped yew and beech hedges, now high enough to disengage the rill gardens from the contrasting world of the grottos.

THE 'ALTO' CASCADES: A NOTE ON DETAIL

It is theoretically possible to create a true harmonic water chord from four cascades, but scientifically speaking it will require as much research as any musical instrument. The Shute cascades are a happy affair of hit or miss, made simply of copper Vs set in concrete. The greater the number of Vs, the more fragmented is the water and therefore the lighter the tone as it falls on the calm water below. This at least is the reasoning, the Vs growing less in number as they move downstream through trebles, altos, tenors and bass.

THE GROTTOS

The silhouette of the twin grottos begins the sequence of red-tiled roofs down to the water. The grottos illustrate an element essential to landscape art. With their black background giving an illusion of depth, they symbolise the divided flow of water either side of the hill. Our intellect knows that in fact the water itself leaves the canal ignominiously through concealed manholes, but our imagination lifts the idea of the flow of water into the heroic. The grottos themselves, influenced by William Kent, are the first backward step in time as we proceed along the perimeter path.

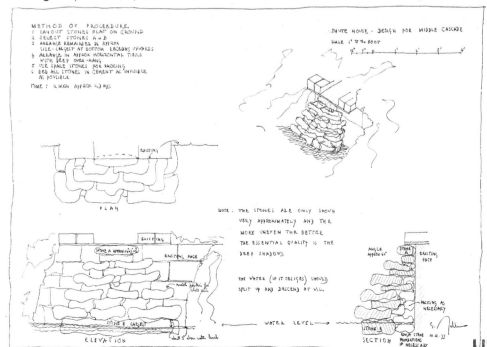

THE KEY PERSPECTIVES

Three views within the garden at Shute appeal especially to Jellicoe and his collaborators, Michael and Anne Tree. In the first, as Jellicoe describes it:

> You are sitting on the two-way seat (before the spring) with your back to the silent pool and spring. Before you are the two routes of the water, the classic and the romantic. The view only shows the tranquil classical canal leading past observation balconies and water lilies to plunge into twin grottos, one for each side of the ridge. Behind the grottos the three Roman poets look down upon these works, and indeed the whole garden. To the right of you, and out of sight, the water has followed a romantic route through a sinister scene of ominous topiary, so to rejoin the classical works at the foot of the cascade.[9]

The second view is that looking up the cascade to the waterfalls and bubble fountains, a view enhanced by the harmonic chords of the upper waterfalls and nature itself. The third, more unexpected route, is where:

> the combined waters pass through [the] bog garden with [its] primaeval sculpture, three huge stones quarried on the site, and the same luxurious wealth of planting that is everywhere. The waters then leave the woodlands and become placid reflecting pools before continuing on their way into infinity. The theory is that the conscious mind will later inform you that you have experienced something intangible that will be unforgettable.[10]

One realises that Jellicoe has chosen these three views because each contains the essence of a particular philosophical aspect that, conjoined with the others, makes up the central message of Shute.

The first *veduta* derives from Jellicoe's preoccupation since early in his career with the debate between Classicism, generally perceived as emanating from the continent, and Romanticism, which Jellicoe considers to represent the English contribution to landscape design prior to the twentieth century:

> The smaller manor houses, farms, hamlets and villages were absorbed in this [eighteenth-century] rural scene, but not the

OPPOSITE: Claude Lorrain, Landscape with Aeneas at Delos. Reproduced by courtesy of the Trustees, The National Gallery, London.

57

estates of the landed aristocracy. The vast, rigidly geometrical patterns with their overwhelming sense of authority were alien to the gently undulating countryside and, to any leader of English thought inspired by the liberalism of Milton and Locke, hopelessly outdated.

Although there had previously been probings into romantic landscape design, notably by Vanbrugh at Castle Howard, the art was crystallised through the circle of poets, painters and architects gathered round the Earl of Burlington. The movement was elite, aristocratic and so unrealistic that it might have been satirised out of existence had not Pope and others recognised its significance, ie that no civilised world of reason can exist without its counterpart of a world of fantasy. From a mathematically proportioned Palladian window, the view was of an idealised pastoral landscape, a figment of the imagination brought to life. You had immersed yourself in Lucretius, Virgil and Ovid, for these poets contained the sum of Classical human feeling towards the countryside and you were enriched by participation in such lofty imagery. Visually you entered the world of the painter.[11]

Taking the vantage point of the double-facing seat by the spring at Shute, the first viewpoint which Jellicoe enjoins us to share with him is really his form of introduction to the two views in landscape design that were so forcibly debated in the eighteenth century, and yet are still in dispute to this day in amended form: He now introduces us to the mythological roots of Romanticism:

Fully to appreciate the most influential painters, Nicolas Poussin and Claude Lorrain, one had to be educated in Classical mythology, with some understanding of its symbols and allegories. This first stimulated interest and thereafter one was drawn into the beautiful scene by all the arts of pictorial composition: foreground, middle distance and a far distance that melted into a luminous sky. Could such a scene, successfully translated from poetry, be translated into real landscape? Was the single viewpoint of the observer an actual restraint on movement, or was it merely a gateway through which the imagination entered the painting and roamed at will? The response was literary as well as pictorial, taking three basic forms: the idealised form, the allegory and the myth. All were a journey into the past. The basic rules of composition were summarised by Pope:

OPPOSITE ABOVE: The Classical View.
OPPOSITE BELOW: The Romantic View.

59

'Consult the Genius of the Place in all,

That tells the Waters or to rise, or fall,

Or helps th' ambitious Hill the Heav'ns to scale,

Or scoops in circling Theatres the Vale,

Calls in the Country, catches opening Glades,

Joins willing Woods, and varies Shades from Shades,

Now breaks, or now directs, the intending Lines,

Paints as you plant, and as you work, Designs.'[12]

The view from the seat is really a *mise-en-scène* arranged by Jellicoe. As he says, water is the subsidiary, but it is also the medium through whose various forms he can now lead us to experience the whole essence of landscape design. Accordingly, the next view with which we are presented is quite different: now we have followed the prescribed romantic route, and we are enjoined to confront the cascade in all its glory. There is harmony too, this time in sound: in the different chords created by the carefully calculated cadences of the falls. That, plus the extended perspective up the rill, past the fountains inspired by a visit to Kashmir. Here is active water, man the master-conductor, and lush planting the backdrop.

We have now experienced the Picturesque and the Beautiful. Jellicoe, knowing that in due course we will come to experience the Sublime, rates the mysterious bog garden as the third most essential viewing experience at Shute, on account of its inevitable effect upon the subconscious mind. To this, at Shute, we will be obliged to return more than once.

Burke conceived the Sublime as an emotion arising solely from horror and astonishment. Both rob the mind of the power to reason and so release the imagination into things unknown.[13]

The Sublime was an experience not immediately apparent in the development of Shute, important as it was, and its attainment eluded Geoffrey Jellicoe and Michael and Anne Tree for at least a decade.

The view out from the bog garden had been so designed that first one pool, through a clearing to the south-east, then a second, combined to lift the eye out of the garden in the direction of the Downs beyond. But by 1988 both the lush undergrowth of the place, and the branches that hemmed it in, had reduced this effect. In early summer the clearing was re-opened again, and Jellicoe had the idea of lifting the perspective, literally to the skies. The addition of a further pool completed the effect dramatically. Edmund Burke was fully vindicated: earth and sky now were united as one.

OPPOSITE: View looking out from the Bog Garden.

Seen from the terrace and lawns between the cedars of Lebanon in front of the house (which after all is the first grand experience the visitor has of the garden and landscape placement) this third pool was also to have an improving effect. Initially Jellicoe had conceived these pools as twin grand pianos:

> I call it the landscape of the two pianos. I was suddenly inspired at a concert by two pianos that could capture a single harmony. So to draw the eye to the view of distant Downs I split the water into two ponds, with the view beyond.[14]

Before that this view had been one of 'those noble views which you weren't supposed to walk in, but only look at from the house'.

We are, as Jellicoe perceived, back in the world of Capability Brown again:

> Lancelot Brown's experience as head gardener under successive architects at Stowe gave him insight into the complex range of classical-romanticism being explored mainly by Kent. From this he distilled the pure abstract form that, with an architect's mind, he detected as underlying all landscape design . . . Probably because it is empty of any ideas beyond the primary, a Brown park is universal and dateless; the landscape could equally well complement a Bauhaus structure as a Palladian one.[15]

Viewed from the front of the house, the third pool simply enhanced and complemented the generalised landscape towards the Downs which existed. Jellicoe uses this to disarm the visitor to the innermost gardens; the pleasures of the Picturesque as a palliative before he introduces reason and debate, on an extraordinary round of visual experiences, culminating in that tantalising glimpse of the Sublime.

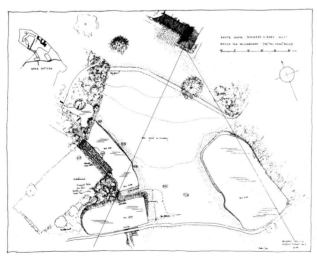

LEFT: The Initial Pools Sequence to the south of Shute House as proposed by Jellicoe to extend the waterscape beyond the grounds.
OPPOSITE: The Bog Garden. Stone placement.

HOW THE GARDEN GREW
PLANTINGS SURVEYED

Only careful analysis of the individual arrays of specialised planting, nurtured and developed over almost two decades at Shute, can reveal the true level of creativity deployed by Michael and Anne Tree. Now in the late summer of 1993, the blooms are at their most impressive, in the truly English tradition.

THE CANAL

The deep profile hedge running along the south edge, inspired perhaps by those at Rousham, is *Fagus sylvatica*. At the amphitheatre, *Buxus sempervirens* is used as a backdrop to the busts of the three Augustan poets. Clumps of lilies (*Zantedeschia aethiopoca*), planted at regular intervals, line the northern edge in profusion. Passing into the small philosophers' grove, to the southerly side, thirteen ilex trees are carefully grown to allow a clear, low view below the branches of their trunks.

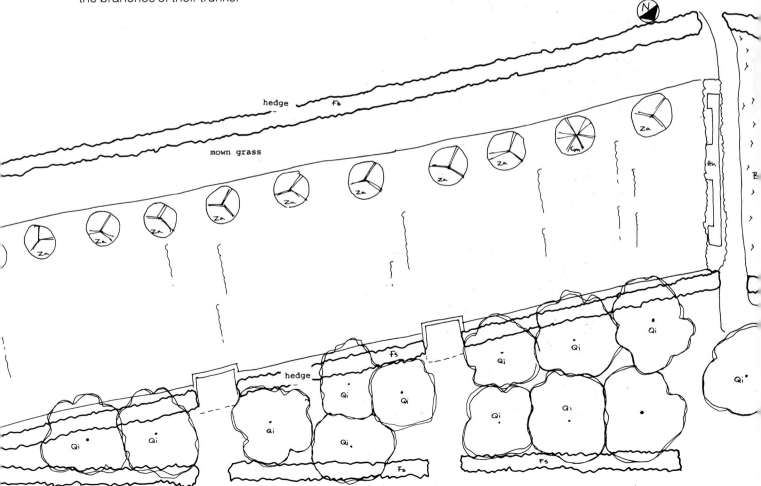

THE TEMPLE GARDEN

This particular garden preoccupied Anne Tree and Jellicoe for some considerable time. On the one hand it relied upon Jellicoe's ideas about 'allegory', consciously expressed; on the other it was a space that undoubtedly preoccupied Anne Tree's subconscious mind to the extent that she drew out a number of sketches. To his credit, Jellicoe has designed a final version that is remarkably close to her original ideas. An essential prerequisite was the high laurel hedge, to maintain surprise at the approaches, and the carefully grown laurel 'tunnel' through which one enters (*Prunus laurocerasus*).

The temple structure is composed of rapidly growing *Hedra helix,* a most suitable ivy species. One of Jellicoe's favourite ilex trees stands in the northerly corner, and seven examples of *Taxus baccata* provide a suitably manageable suggestion of standing figures (with clipped heads) which both client and architect wanted to create. In the north-westerly corner the steeple is growing on its steel frame, clad in *Tsuga heterophylla*: the floor of this garden is covered in gravel, but the approaches to the temple have steps and flooring of tree sections. This extraordinary space was developed between 1988 and 1993 and together with the third pool in the view from the bog garden it represents the final flourish of its creators. As the next decade passes, providing the Garden Allegory is maintained properly, it will grow to maturity as a permanent reminder of their productive collaboration in plumbing the recesses of the subconscious mind.

OPPOSITE FROM ABOVE TO BELOW, L TO R: The Laurel Tunnel (Prunus laurocerasus), entry point; Laurel Hedge; the Temple clad in ivy (Hedra helix); the iron frames for the topiary figures (Taxus baccata). BELOW: Planting Survey of the Temple Garden, Key to Plants: Buxus sempervirens; Hedra helix; Prunus laurocerasus; Quercus ilex; Taxus baccata; Tilia cordata; Tsuga heterophylla.

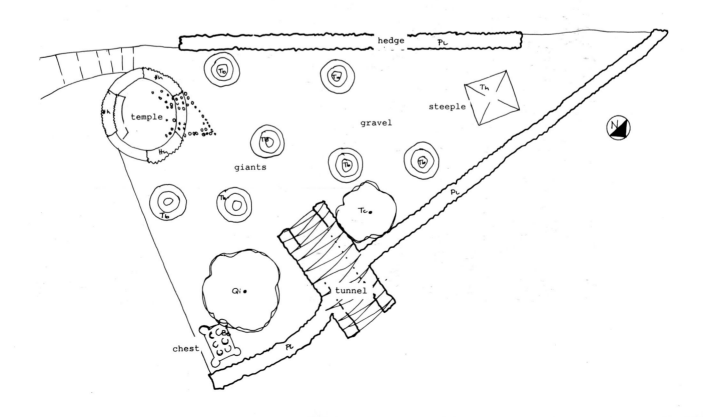

THE BOX GARDEN

The six planted beds of regular square plan, surrounded by box borders of workable height, are basically divided into four beds for flowers or shrubs and two for fruit and vegetables. In the first four, *Malus sylvestris* forms a centrepiece. There is an emphasis on early summer blooms, even in springtime: *Aconitum napellus* is then a pleasant surprise. Generally, chrysanthemums, delphiniums, geraniums, peonies and irises proliferate. There are four species of geranium: *dalmaticum*, *endressii*, *pratense* and 'Johnson's Blue'. (The more detailed dispositions are given in the planting plan.) In 1993, raspberry canes filled the fifth bed, and cabbage, potatoes and rhubarb the sixth. The overall impression is one of practical plant husbandry, combined with essential kitchen provisions. Lady Anne Tree's design for the planting brims with originality and one can spend much time deciphering the variously juxtaposed blooms.

OPPOSITE FROM ABOVE TO BELOW, L TO R: Box Beds, general view to show varied planting; Box Beds: note canes indicating location of fruit and vegetable planting; Box Bed planted with vegetables; Box Bed planted with a mixture of annuals and perennial species.
BELOW: Planting Survey of the Box Garden, Key to Plants: Achemilla mollis; Aconitum napellus; Buxus sempervirens; Chrysanthemum maximim; Delphinium ajacis; Euphorbia polochroma; Geranium dalmaticum; Geranium endressii; Geranium pratense; Geranium 'Johnson's Blue'; Iris sibirica; Lychnis coronaria; Malus sylvestris; Malva alcea 'Fastigiata'; Nicotiana sanderae; Onopordum acanthium; Paeonia lactiflora officinalis; Pelargonium quercifolium; Tagetes tenuifolia; Trollius cultorum 'Orange Princess'.

mown grass

hedge

THE RILL

The rill at Shute forms the centrepiece of the whole project. It is the pinnacle of the successful collaboration and, conceived in the 1970s, represents that aspect of the whole place which has now reached a full fruition in terms of successful planting and good husbandry.

Geoffrey Jellicoe laid out the bones of the rill and its detailed cascades with their harmonic sound effects. However, the complex planting out of the twelve main divisions of space through which the watercourse passes (in three stages of level) before moving through mown grass, was wholly devised by the Trees. There is great subtlety too in the containment of scale – flattering the scale of the whole venture. Rose trees have grown up in the life span of the project and occupy strategic positions. *Lonicera* marks the key entry point from the house lawns. Some fifty named plants fill what is by any standards a somewhat modest area, and are designated in the plant survey.

The lower reaches of the rill are planted with abundant clumps of *Hosta sieboldiana*, *Hosta crispula* and *Hosta fortunei* 'Albopicta' which take full advantage of the moisture: while further up is a mass of Fireglow (*Euphorbia griffithii*). Wisteria is seen growing through tree foliage. Roses are carefully restricted to the deep red *Rosa arvensis* and the white *Rosa canina*. Geraniums, peonies, narcissi, irises and primula abound. Throughout spring and summer there is an exotic colouring which survives until autumn.

OPPOSITE FROM ABOVE TO BELOW, L TO R: The Cascade in operation (author's photograph); Wisteria sinensis trained over an arch; deep planting around the upper section of the Rill; Honeysuckle. BELOW: Planting Survey of the Rill, Key to Plants: Achemilla mollis; Agapanthus 'Headbourne Hybrids'; Beriberis gyalacia; Beriberis thunbergii atropurpurea; Butomus umbellatus; Buxus sempervirens; Caltha palustis; Chamaecyparis lawsoniana 'Fletcheri'; Convallaria masalis; Cornus alba; Cyperus longus; Doronicum caucasicum; Endymion non-scritpus; Euphorbia griffithii 'Fireglow'; Fatsia japonica; Fagus sylvatica; Geranium endressii; Hamamelis mollis; Hebe cupressoides; Hosta crispula; Hosta fortunei 'Albopicta'; Hosta sieboldiana; Hosta 'Thomas Hogg'; Hosta undulata; Iris sibirica; Ligularia stenocephata; Lonicera periclymenum; Lysichitum americanum; Magnolia soulangiana; Myosotis sylvatica; Narcissus 'Actaea'; Paeonia lutea var ludlowii; Phyllitis scolopendrium; Primula sp; Prunus lusitanica; Rodgersia tabularis; Rosa arvensis; Rosa canina; Salix fragilis; Saxifraga umbrosa; Symphytum grandiflorum; Taxus baccata; Verbascum bombyciferum; Virbinum furcatum; Virbinum opulus 'Sterile'; Wisteria sinensis.

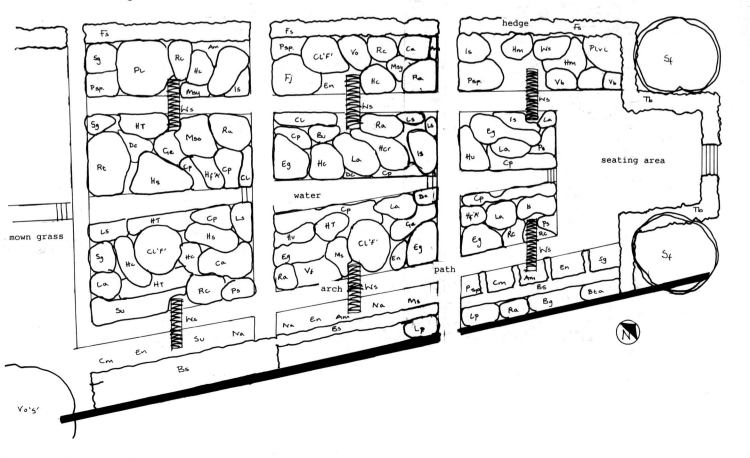

THE BOG GARDEN

The bog garden is so lush, almost equatorial in its late summer humidity, that the massive *Gunnera manicata* can intimidate the diminutive in spirit, as they merge with the undergrowth surrounding the Zimbabwean sentinel sculpture as a subtle antidote to the physical and mental exposure forced by the allegorical garden and its high temple. However, here again springs a variety of *hosta*, predominantly *fortunei* 'Albopicta' with its pale blue tints. The three important stones to which Jellicoe attaches much importance lie surrounded by *Lysichitum americanum*, *Iris sibirica*, and *Dryopteris cristata*; *Rhododendron ponticum* is also allowed in, a reminder of its earlier abundance close to the spring source.

OPPOSITE FROM ABOVE TO BELOW, L TO R: Wild species proliferate in the Bog Garden, and the gunnera flourishes; Iris sibirica; Gunnera manicata; hostas and Iris sibirica.
BELOW: Planting Survey of the Bog Garden, Key to Plants: Acer pseudoplatanus; Cortaderia selloana; Corylus avallana; Dryopteris cristata; Epilobium hirsutum; Endymion non-scriptus; Galium odoratum; Geranium enderssii; Geranium robertianum; Gunnera manicata; Helleborus viridis; Hosta crispula; Hosta fortunei 'Albopicta'; Hosta sieboldiana; Hosta 'Thomas Hogg'; Hosta undulata; Iris sibirica; Phyllitis scolopendrium; Primula sp; Rhododendron ponticum; Salix caprea; Sorbus aucuparia; Stellaria holostea; Symphytum uplandicum; Taraxcum officinale; Veronica officinalis; Viburnum lentago; Lysichitum americanum.

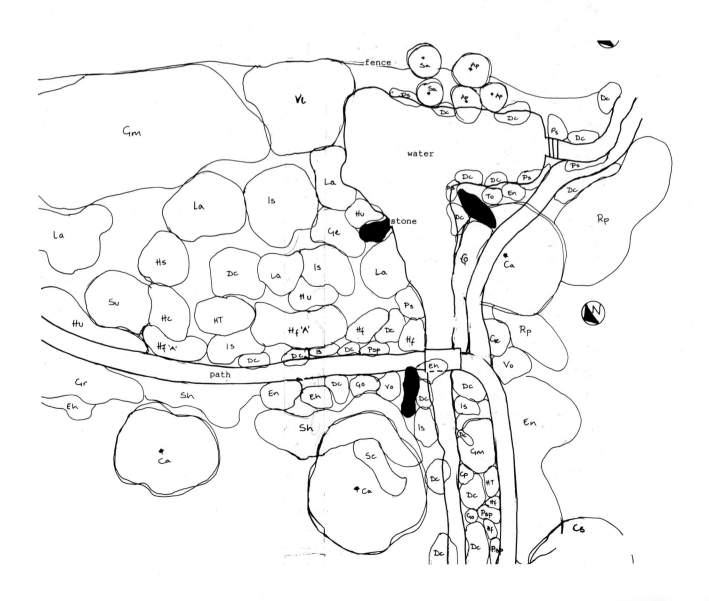

THE SPRING

Finally, the spring pool, beginning and end of the entire raison d'etre of the gardens, and source of the water courses, is beneficiary of a carefully modulated planting plan that fuses artifice with wilderness. Close in, camellias contrast with the deep green underwater rocks. *Dryopteris cristata* marks the bounds of this pool in some eight areas; and *Hosta* 'Thomas Hogg' defines the entrance and access to this small area. The powerful growth of *Rhododendron ponticum*, largely unconstrained, provides an effective screen to this discreet, mysterious zone overall, filling the southern lake edge, and surrounding the two-way seat, all south of the main path of access. But only *Betula pendula* vies with it to the north.

OPPOSITE FROM ABOVE TO BELOW, L TO R: Gap at the approach to the Spring; the Spring; Rhododendron ponticum; View out from the gap at the Spring Source.
BELOW: Planting Survey of the Spring, Key to Plants: Betula pendula; Camellia japonica 'Erin Farmer'; Camellia japonica 'Grand Slam'; Camellia reticulata 'Confucius'; Dryopteris cristata; Hosta 'Thomas Hogg'; Prunus laurocerasus; Rhododendron ponticum.

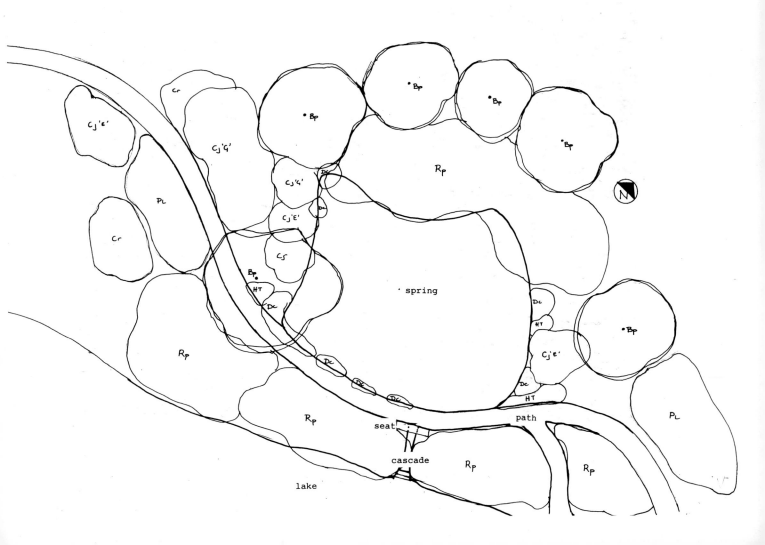

FAREWELL TO SHUTE

As the l990s got under way, the garden at Shute became the centre of increasing attention from the press, the media and from the landscape and gardening professionals and enthusiasts. During 1991 an energetic television team under Roger Last (BBC *Omnibus*) had assembled a unique documentary on the life and work of Sir Geoffrey Jellicoe. Screened one Sunday evening in February 1992 mid-evening, it was calculated by the BBC to have rated eleven million viewers. While it documented all the major works that Jellicoe had accomplished by then, it was clear to the audience that the garden 'laboratory' at Shute, with its remarkable water schema, offered a complete résumé of what Jellicoe was really about. There followed additional television coverages on Shute, and by 1992 Michael and Anne Tree realised that Shute had indeed reached superstar status among gardens.

In the late summer of that year Jellicoe himself paid what he described as a last visit; not that he was himself letting up: he was in the midst of designing his last major project to date, the Historical Gardens for Atlanta, plus two more substantial private projects. In the balmy evening air of that perfect evening, the Trees had arranged to have dinner with their guest on the terrace at the head of the cascade and rill. Now they could all relax, three very creative people who knew that they could neither add nor take away from the completed work – not in fact a condition particularly suited to any of their restless temperaments. But the work was done. Invited down again in 1993, Jellicoe said that last evening had been so sublime that he could really survive on the memory. The menu is not recorded. Jellicoe said that it was not just the splendour of the blooms, and their gentle scent in the air, nor the perfect company: but it was also the harmony of sounds; the soft descant of the cascade, the rustle of the ilex leaves over the hedge, the deeper note of the breeze in the great beech.

It had been a long collaboration, and it had formed the background to a period which represented the full flowering of the landscape architect's own career. Ironically, but significantly, this had all happened since his official retirement and the dispersal of the office.

OPPOSITE: The View down the Canal from the two-way seat.

ABOVE: View from the Terrace, essentially a point of arrival, down the Rill and Cascades, to the small figure sculpture (also from Mereworth).
The Cape Cod chairs are a reminder of the Trees' transatlantic connections.

Firstly had come the commission to design the gardens for Sutton Place, Surrey (1980). This had been almost immediately followed by work on an urban park for the city of Modena,[16] adjacent to Vittorio Gregotti's new housing. This had also boasted a canal, running the length of the scheme, and christened by the Italians the 'Long Water'. In 1981 initial ideas from Jellicoe had been solicited for an urban agrarian park for Brescia in Northern Italy. Virgil had been the inspiration for Modena; now it was Ovid at Brescia, manifested in the design of artificial hills in the form of fish (not a shoal, but as served at his hosts' dinner, caught in Lake Isoe, in five different species); this idea of Ovid's *Metamorphoses* failed quite to catch on with the clients. But following a further, and superb water-related scheme for Sir John Baring's house, The Grange, in Hampshire, a massive new commission materialised in 1984, that for the Botanical Gardens for the Moody Foundation at Galveston, Texas, facing the Gulf of Mexico. Here a series of water routes and vistas characterised the scheme, derived from Lucretius. From that poet's work, *De Rerum Natura*, Jellicoe had found described the nature and origin of the Universe, including humanity itself. Thus the scheme was to offer no human history as such, simply an entirely botanical universe, a hymn to creativity. While the clients considered this scheme unviable in terms of visitor numbers, Jellicoe was not down for long. In 1985 there emerged from the Highgate drawing board a second thematic landscape project; but this time it was based on the *Landscape of Man*, and represented a complete history of Garden Design.

During the resolution of this difficult transition, Jellicoe had been much inspired by the progress at Shute. The Moody Historical Gardens had emerged from the inspiration of the combination of gardens at Shute. The Gardens have now begun on site in Galveston, but their conception was at Shute.

Later, in 1988, Jellicoe worked on an invited project for a leisure and recreational park on the edge of Turin. Here again he offered two remarkable, yet differing schemes of a similar genesis. The (1992) garden design for Sheikh Mansour, in Cairo, deploys a series of water features that culminate in a grove of palm trees.[17] And in that same year, there came the great project for the city of Atlanta, in the form of an American historical gardens sequence with universal ramifications.[18] Heraclitus, the ancient Greek philosopher, was Jellicoe's historical inspiration here. But in the sequence of routes and views, and the use of available water resources, much of the layout is

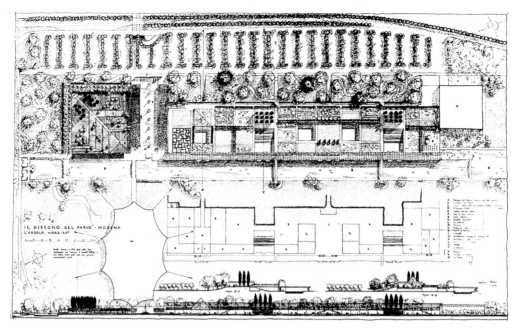

IL DISEGNO DEL PARCO · MODENA
L'ANGOLO NORD-EST

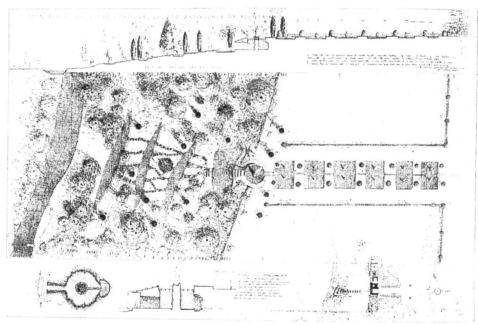

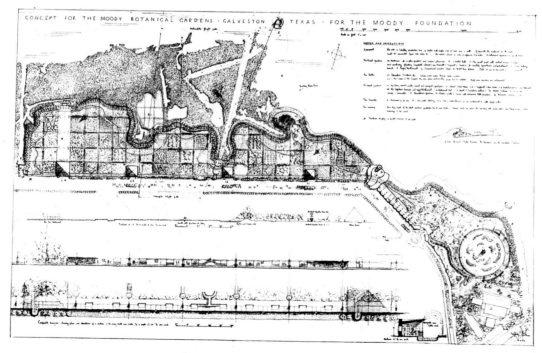

CONCEPT FOR THE MOODY BOTANICAL GARDENS · GALVESTON · TEXAS · FOR THE MOODY · FOUNDATION

NOTES AND OBSERVATIONS

reminiscent of Shute. Jellicoe is still developing the design, due to be completed in time for the 1996 Olympic celebrations at Atlanta City. Of the Garden of Heraclitus there, Jellicoe said:

I hope that the 21st-century 'quiet' garden of contemplation may stir the thoughts to ponder on the past not as the past but as a pointer to the future.

In July 1993, as Jellicoe worked on Atlanta and other projects, the garden gate at Shute was finally closed, and Michael and Anne Tree handed over to a new and caring ownership. Shute remains a private garden and it seems will be maintained in its ultimate condition for many years. In the history of gardens, that is as much as anyone can hope for. Most especially so, in this garden where landscape history was made.

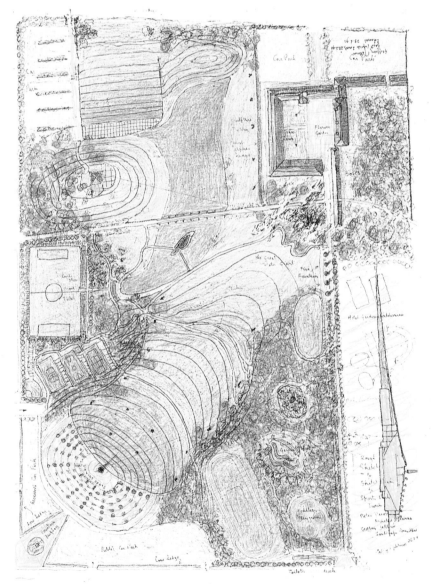

LEFT: The Sports Park and Centre proposals prepared by Jellicoe for Turin (1990), second scheme.
OPPOSITE FROM ABOVE: A Civic Park for Modena – the 'Long Water' runs from left to right across the centre of this drawing of the scheme prepared by Jellicoe in 1984 for the City authorities of Modena, Italy; Sutton Place – the cascade proposed by Jellicoe in 1981 but never executed; Moody Foundation Gardens, Galveston, Texas – Botanical Gardens, first scheme.

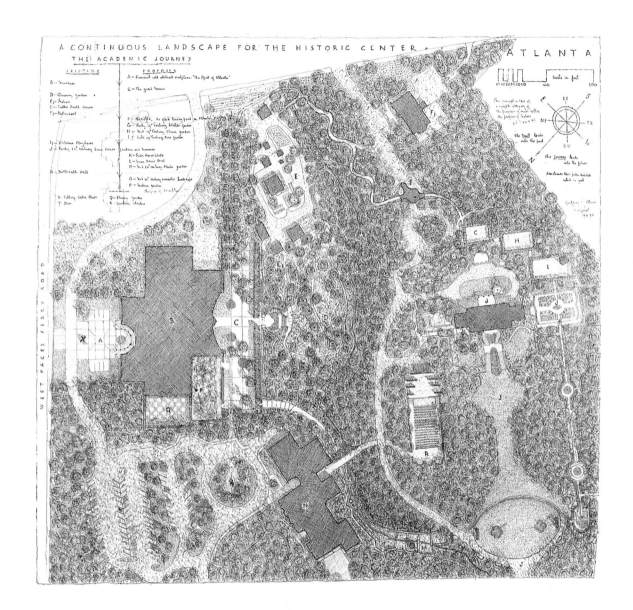

SHUTE AND BEYOND

AN INTERVIEW WITH GEOFFREY JELLICOE

Geoffrey Jellicoe began work at Shute in 1969 and by 1996, a generation later, he will have realised his last great scheme of a career which spans three generations: the gardens for the Atlanta History Centre, Atlanta, USA. In interviewing Geoffrey Jellicoe the importance of the 'landscape laboratory' at Shute in the formulation of this design concept became clearer than ever. In addition to this another of the great inspirations for the final Atlanta scheme turned out to be the work (such as it remains) of the ancient Greek philosopher, Heraclitus (500 BC). To precede the interview, Sir Geoffrey has allowed us to quote from his writing on Heraclitus:

> The declaration of Heraclitus that all things were in flux could not be denied – indeed it was obvious – and it was to provide a sense of stability essential to the human race that Plato evolved the theory of ideas. Plato the mathematician and Aristotle the biologist were concerned only with rational thought and pure reason. They opposed myth and mysticism, and the subconscious as a scientific study and source of deduction did not come their way. Deduction from observation conceived the cosmos to be mathematical, absolute and eternal. The circle, where the end is the beginning, was the mother figure. Could not this divine concept be transmitted to earth to breathe divinity into man's work? Pythagoras had already discovered an affinity between the music of the spheres and that of man, and why not with the other arts? Hence were evolved those abstract mathematical proportions that fill us with wonder, reassurance and placidity. The rub is that today things are not what had been imagined. Plato's noble conception of a metaphysical link between man and eternity has been broken by the scientist. Can the artist repair and renew the link?

> All artists are subconsciously struggling to reach the perfection that is not of this world. The Romantic artist seeks for it in things on earth or in the clouds above; the Classical artist has sought for it in the cosmos beyond the skies. Now that the conception of cosmic stability is no more, to what ends are the

OPPOSITE: This design for Atlanta, the climax of Geoffrey Jellicoe's long career, incorporates much of the thinking behind the Shute garden, albeit on a vastly greater scale. The genesis of many of the elements detailed on the project drawing arose from particular areas developed over twenty-five years at Shute, linked together as a whole by visitor circulation arrangements themselves related to water schemata. The project is intended to be completed in time for the 1996 Olympic Games celebration in the same city.

ABOVE: The Spring Source, Shute.

artists groping? Can Romanticism, the art of change, metamorphose itself into an art that can be called cosmic?

And so we come to Heraclitus, to the grove in which we are sitting, to the adventure in cosmic landscape art that we have just experienced, and to his words of wisdom and encouragement that made it possible.

Although the site at Atlanta is buried in trees, the effect upon the mind of the juxtaposition in the landscape of objects of various kinds was disturbing. The first Heraclitian thought to present itself was paramount: 'The unconscious harmonises with the conscious.' Such a statement seems not to have been made again until Jung. There followed : 'Unity is possible if there are opposites.' But how, for example, can this come about when the neo-Italian Renaissance mansion and the great new museum now being built are so obviously antagonistic? Then came the hidden clue, concealed in the famous words: 'All things are in flux.' Was it possible for the first time in the history of environment to create consciously a subconscious emotional force that would itself be more lasting in the subconscious than would static architecture? Could the Way be more significant than the Stops? Could it become a metaphysical journey in time and space, whose 'Beginnings and ends are shared in the circumference of a circle'? We have ourselves returned to where we began. We have retained Plato's great dictum that all art must be in correspondence with the cosmos; nor have we forgotten that the most stable civilisation in history, Egypt, waits upon a river into which you cannot step twice.

The following interview took place with Geoffrey Jellicoe after the news that the project for a landscape park for Atlanta had been finally confirmed to proceed in time for the 1996 Olympic Games in the city of Atlanta, and following the news that Shute had passed to new ownership.

MS Can you explain the effect of Shute coming into your life (as a project in 1969), both personally and in terms of your work, and how soon did you realise what its significance might be for you ?

GJ The place and its qualities attracted me immediately, and I told Michael and Anne Tree as much. Water was present in abun-

ABOVE: The Stream flowing from the Spring.

ABOVE: The Canal, a feature which already existed in 1969, but which was modified by Jellicoe.

dance, and flowing from the highest level – something which one rarely finds on any site. As the site was a complete jungle at the time, we slowly cleared the ground first.

MS In what state was the long holding pool which eventually became the canal, the most important feature at the top of the site?

GJ We actually shortened this, in order to provide additional accommodation for staff (behind the present busts of the poets). At one point I considered that the guest rooms should be there on account of the potential view down the canal, but this was impractical. The present solution has worked much better.

MS The garden at Shute, as a whole, then continued to evolve for almost quarter of a century?

GJ Yes. The cascade was included in the very first plans, and from then on the Trees and I advanced side by side, so to speak: they would propose an idea, I would look at the reality of it. The planting was entirely Anne's. It was not as if a professional plantsman (such as the late Lanning Roper) came there. Roper rather looked down on us all. No one was appointed as such. Anne decided absolutely everything in this respect, hence the wildness of it, which I love – completely attuned to my own philosophy – and this is also grand.

MS On a grand scale?

GJ Exactly. Anne feels with the architecture there that they are a part of the garden as does Michael, and could not accept the solution that would be imposed by a Lanning Roper type of designer or planting expert – so the design proceeded in stages – just the three of us interpreting what lay in our minds, gradually over twenty or so years.

MS So now, looking back a generation, in view of the major projects such as Sutton Place and Modena – the urban landscape park – and then the first and second Moody Foundation schemes at Galveston and finally Atlanta, can you trace any specific influence which Shute has had as a kind of laboratory for your ideas?

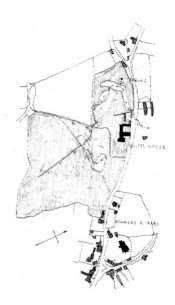

ABOVE: The Water Scheme as finally developed: the Spring and Canal can be seen at the top right.
OPPOSITE: View from the Rill looking towards the Cascade.

ABOVE: The end of the Canal with busts of the three Roman poets.

GJ Well, it's very hard to pin down the absolutely direct and specific influences in this way. But then one thinks of the effect of the subconscious mind – which of course I am very influenced by in terms of effect – and obviously, behind everything, Shute had a great affect. Atlanta in a way has been the closest to Shute in rhythm – and in movement. The rapid movement of water at Shute, rushing down and through and then seemingly disappearing into the sky – this has a parallel in the controlling force of continual movement evident in the Atlanta scheme. So in exploring the deeper side of landscape design, Shute was the precursor.

MS Now referring to your 1992 paper on Jung for the Museum of Modern Art, New York, how important does Jung seem in the period from the 1980s onwards?

GJ Well, very. But how much of Jung's theories actually came to be applied is not very certain. Yes, he was sort of hovering around. But there was no intellectualising at Shute. The design came out in a very pure, instinctive way – with the Trees too. Anything too intellectual in application would have spoiled this. Of course later on Jung's influence was felt at Galveston, and even before that, at Sutton Place: but never at Shute. I remember the time that [Henry] Moore came across some Jung and said: 'I mustn't read any more, it will get in the way of my instincts.' I too felt the same here as Henry did. The problem is that the intellect can start 'buzzing around', and I think that keeping this down kept Shute 'pure' and it remained so.

MS So Shute remained authentic in this way.

GJ Of course the intellectual contribution can have a good effect up to a point. At the moment I am back studying the Roman poets, and Horace and so on, and one does see and value the involvement of scholarship as such.

MS Here it was the canal that played an important part? One can look outwards from the two-way seat, one of your key views, in front of the spring source, a wide view down the poets' canal in a north-easterly direction, and then switch southwards and catch the

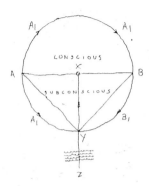

ABOVE: Post Jungian diagram indicating Jellicoe's concept of the creative process in the design of landscape (1988).
A   Client
A1   Client instruction
B   Designer
B1   Designer's initial concept
Y   Joint subconscious
Z   Deep subconscious of both
X   Final design solution

ABOVE: The view towards Shute House from the two-way seat.

Romantic landscape there with its classical sculptured figure, yet which makes no intellectual claims whatever.

GJ The involvement somewhere of scholarship creates a sense of historical depth – as Shakespeare knew.

GJ The richness of Shute derives I suppose from the combination of some scholarship, providing that sense of depth, together with the action of the subconscious mind in the design process and the involvement in that way too of the two clients, Anne and Michael Tree.

MS Who were, it seems, absolutely confident about the direction in which you were all moving.

GJ Yes, they slowly pushed ahead over the years – sometimes they were slightly off beat and then I immediately steered them back in terms of what was practical or realisable. Yet they always allowed me to solve things in my own way, as with the three poet figures at the head of the canal.

MS And this all seems to work on several levels.

GJ Yes, that seems to be so.

MS So when one now looks at the scheme accepted for Atlanta, one can not help feeling that Heraclitus might have a place at Shute too.

GJ Well of course that is rather nearer to the Roman period that the Greek philosopher comes – but yes – he would immediately understand the sense of movement created by the flowing waters, and that sound . . .

MS Of flowing water? One remembers the Heraclitean saying that one cannot jump into the same river twice.

GJ (laughs) . . . and all things being in flux, yes.

FOOTNOTES

1 *The Italian Gardens of the Renaissance*, Geoffrey Jellicoe and JC Shepherd, London, 1925.

2 *The Landscape of Man*, Geoffrey and Susan Jellicoe, London and New York, 1975.

3 *Studies in Landscape Design*, Geoffrey Jellicoe, 3 Volumes 1960-70, Oxford.

4 *Water: The Use of Water in Landscape Architecture*, Geoffrey and Susan Jellicoe, London and New York, 1971.

5 *Ibid.*

6 Interview with P Sullivan, *Sunday Times Magazine*, 1991.

7 *Denatured Visions: Landscape and Culture in the Twentieth Century*, edited by Stuart Wrede and William Howard Adams. *Cf* essay by Geoffrey Jellicoe 'Jung and the Art of Landscape', p127, Museum of Modern Art, New York, 1991.

8 These descriptions were first given in *The Guelph Lectures on Landscape Design*, University of Guelph (Canada), 1983, pp8-23, with the exception of the 'Temple Garden Revised' which first appeared in an interview with L Geddes-Brown, *House and Garden*, 1991.

9 Jellicoe Papers (unpublished), 1991.

10 *Ibid.*

11 *Ibid* (1984).

12 *Ibid*, Jellicoe quotes Alexander Pope, 'An Epistle to Lord Burlington' (1731).

13 *Ibid.*

14 *Op cit*, note 7.

15 Interview with the author, January 1989.

16 Professor Leonardo Benevolo, the leading Italian architect, town planner and historian, was instrumental in the consideration of Jellicoe for this commission.

17 Project now under development in Cairo (August 1993).

18 Jellicoe drew initially on Bertrand Russell (*History of Western Philosophy*), subsequently on Sir Karl Popper (*The Open Society and Its Enemies*, Volume 1: Plato, Chapter 2 Heraclitus) for guidance. At an early stage in the design he concluded that Heraclitus had a greater bearing on the concept than Plato and so re-arranged a grove initially as 'of Plato' in the name of Heraclitus. Jellicoe extended his study of the pre-Socratic philosopher to include the original text *On Nature* as translated in the *Fragments* (Bywater 1877), to verify the doctrine of universal flux as propounded by Heraclitus.

BIOGRAPHY

Geoffrey Alan Jellicoe was born in London on 8 October 1900 and educated at the Architectural Association School, London, 1919-23 (Bernard Webb Scholarship, Neale Bursary). He received the Dip AA in 1923. He married Susan Jellicoe (formerly Susan Pares) in 1936. Jellicoe was in partnership with JC Shepherd as Shepherd & Jellicoe Architects in London 1925-31; in practice on his own from 1931-38; a senior partner (with the garden designers Russell Page and Richard Wilson) as Jellicoe, Page and Wilson, London 1938-39; as principal of GA Jellicoe, London 1939-58; and a senior partner (with Alan Ballantyne and Francis Coleridge) in Jellicoe, Ballantyne and Coleridge, London, 1964-73.

From 1929-34 Jellicoe was a Studio Master at the Architectural Association School, London, and from 1939-42 its Principal. In 1929 he was a founder member of the Institute of Landscape Architects and from 1939-49 its President; from 1948-54 he was Founder President of the International Federation of Landscape Architects and has been Honorary Life President since 1954. He was a member of the Royal Fine Art Commission (1954-68) and a Trustee of the Tate Gallery (1967-74). He was a recipient of the American Institute of Landscape Architects Medal in 1991. He is an Associate RIBA; an Honorary Corresponding Member of the American Society of Landscape Architects and the Venezuelan Society of Landscape Architects. He received a CBE in 1963 and was knighted in 1979. In 1991 he was elected a Member of the Royal Academy of Arts.

As the following list of those landscape and garden projects which Jellicoe considers most significant suggests, he has practised landscape design continuously from 1925 until today. He is currently at work on the detailed design for the Historical Landscape Park at Atlanta City. Geoffrey Jellicoe has also been engaged as an author on works covering aspects of landscape and garden design since 1925.

THE LANDSCAPE AND GARDEN DESIGNS
OF GEOFFREY JELLICOE 1929-93

1929-34	Village Plan, Broadway, Gloucestershire
1934-38	Visitors Centre, Cheddar Gorge, Somerset
1936-39	Terrace/Garden, Royal Lodge, Windsor
1939/47	Garden Design, Sandringham, Norfolk
1935	Stanmore
1935	Garden Design, Ditchley Park, Oxfordshire
1936	Garden Design, The Holme, Regents Park, London
1936-89	Appraisals, revisions to layouts, restoration, St Pauls Walden Bury, Hertfordshire
1942-88	Landscape Design and Conservation Plan, Hope Cement Works, Peak District
1941	Newport
1946	Landscape Plan and Recreational Centre, Mablethorpe, Lincolnshire
1947-59	Town Landscaped Park, Hemel Hempsted, Hertfordshire
1947-52	Plan and Hotel Design, Lusaka, Africa
1949-52	Walsall Memorial Gardens, West Midlands
1949-79	Binghams Melcombe, Somerset
1955	Landscape Plan, Nottingham University
1956	Harveys Roof Garden, Guildford
1957	Civic and Market Hall, Totnes, Devon
1957	Ruskin Drive, St Helens
1959	Landscape Plan, Guinness Co, Park Royal, Middlesex
1960	Landscape Plan, Harwell, Berkshire
1960	Landscape Plan, Oldbury Power Station, Avon
1961	Conservation Plan, Gloucester
1962	Rose Garden, Cliveden, Buckinghamshire
1963	Crystal Span (Thames Bridge), London
1963	Landscape Plan, Christ Church Meadow, Oxford
1964	Kennedy Memorial, Runnymede, Berkshire
1964	Development Plan, Tollcross, Edinburgh
1965	Garden Design, Horsted, Sussex
1966	Building Design and Environs, Grantham Crematorium, Lincolnshire
1967	Garden Design, Armagh Cathedral, Northern Ireland
1967	Landscape Design, Isle of Sark
1968	Landscape Design and Building Plans, Cheltenham
1969-88	Garden Design, Shute
1971-75	Landscape Design, Stratford-on-Avon
1972	Chequers
1972	Fitzroy Square, London
1972-74	Landscape Design, New Palace Yard, Westminster
1973	Pools Design, Royal Horticultural Society, Wisley
1974	Cathedral Steps, Exeter
1974	Everton Park, Bedfordshire
1975	Garden Design, Baring House, Hampshire
1980	Garden Design and Restoration, Hartwell House, Buckinghamshire
1980	Garden Design, Sutton Place, Guildford
1980	Landscape and Urban Park, Modena, Italy
1981	Landscape Agrarian Park, Brescia, Italy
1983-	Moody Gardens, Galveston, Texas
1988	Villa at Asolo, Italy
1989-90	Leisure Park, Turin
1989-90	Garden Design, Tidcombe Manor, Wiltshire
1991	Danemere Park
1992	Garden for Sheik Mansour, Cairo
1992	Garden at Denbies, near Woking, Surrey
1992-93	Historical Gardens, Atlanta